50 Flashcards $8.95

FlashCards

8th Grade
The Ohio
Achievement
Test

SOCIAL STUDIES
Preparing Students for the OAT

Printed in USA. Minimal packaging for a healthy environment.
©2008 Hollandays Publishing Corporation

HOLLANDAYS
Publishing Corporation

1) What was the **Renaissance?**

2) What was the main effect of
the **Reformation?**

1

1) **Renaissance** = Arts, education, ideas
   The Renaissance was a revival or rebirth of interest in the arts and education in Europe in the 1500s and early 1600s (16th and early 17th Centuries).

2) **Reformation** = Changes in church
   The Reformation brought important changes to the Christian church in Europe. Protestant churches were formed to protest against some practices of the Catholic church in the 1500s (16th Century).

1) Define the following terms.
   a) B.C. (B.C.E.)
   b) A.D. (C.E.)

2) Which date comes first on a timeline?
   480 B.C. or A.D. 320

1) a) before Christ, refers to events before Christ's birth (before the common era)

   b) *Anno Domini*, (in the year of our Lord) refers to events after Christ's birth (common era)

2) 480 B.C.

1) What is **imperialism?**

2) What is a **colony?**

3) What is the result of imperialism?

1) **Imperialism** is a policy used by strong nations to control and profit from weaker nations.

2) The nation or territory that is dominated by a strong nation is a **colony**.

3) The strong nation prospers as it is enriched by the resources of the colony. The colony may lose its culture or language as a result of changes made by the strong nation.

Match the civilization with its description.
Rome or **Egypt**

1) experimented with limited democracy

2) built the pyramids

3) developed effective methods to preserve the dead

4) built large network of straight stone roads to support military campaigns

1) **Rome**: experimented with limited democracy

2) **Egypt**: built the pyramids

3) **Egypt**: developed effective methods to preserve the dead

4) **Rome**: built large network of straight stone roads to support military campaigns

Identify the culture that produced each contribution.

India, China, or Greece

1) recognized that Earth was a sphere rotating on its axis and revolving around the Sun

2) developed drama and built temples

3) created a terra cotta army of thousands of soldiers

1) **India:** recognized that Earth was a sphere rotating on its axis and revolving around the sun

2) **Greece:** developed drama and built temples

3) **China:** created a terra cotta army of thousands of soldiers

List five effects the Crusades had on Europe.

- Islamic thought influenced the West.
- Building materials changed.
- Roads carried more traffic.
- It aided the beginning of the Renaissance in Italy.
- Military expansion of Islam slowed.

What are some differences between the lifestyles of the Paleolithic Era and the lifestyles of the Neolithic Era?

People in the Paleolithic Era were hunters and gatherers and moved from place to place for food. People in the Neolithic Era developed farming societies, slowing the need for migration and enabling the rise of permanent civilizations.

Match the civilization with its description.
Aztec or Inca

1) Which civilization expanded from the area of modern day Peru?

2) Which empire based its religion on the Sun?

3) Which civilization was located in the area of modern day Mexico?

4) Which empire included human sacrifices in its religious rites?

1) Inca
2) Inca
3) **Aztec**
4) **Aztec**

1) Define urbanization.

2) Define deforestation.

3) Can urbanization lead to deforestation? Explain.

1) urbanization: more people moving to cities

2) deforestation: the destruction of areas of forest without replanting trees

3) Yes. Land is often cleared for new buildings when cities grow. Forests are destroyed.

1) What are the four factors of production?

2) How might each change below affect production and price of this year's highest selling sports car?

   A) a strike by workers that build the car

   B) a competitor comes out with a similar car

   C) a new color is offered that no other car maker has.

1) Land, labor, capital, entrepreneurship

2) **A)** A labor shortage would hamper production and cause price to go up.

B) Competition gives more choices for consumers and typically means a lower price.

C) Scarcity would cause the price to go up if there was a demand for that color.

Compare and contrast how citizens participate in the following types of democracy:

1) direct democracy

2) representative democracy

1) In a direct democracy, citizens vote directly for laws and rulers, with the principle of "one person, one vote."

2) In a representative democracy, citizens elect representatives to govern the country.

1) Define **Dictatorship**

2) Compare and contrast a dictator and an absolute monarch.

1) **Dictatorship** - a system of government in which one strong ruler controls all governmental powers; dictators often gain control following military victories.

2) Dictators and absolute monarchs both exercise total control over their nations. Dictators take control by force. Absolute monarchs take power when they replace a parent or other family member as ruler.

Match the European power to the practice or location of the colony.

1) set up trading posts to buy and ship furs

2) founded St. Augustine, Florida

3) granted land for a prison colony in Georgia

4) colonies' economic focus was on ranching and mining

5) built outposts on Great Lakes and Mississippi River

6) elected assemblies and governors had weak link to European power

A) Spanish

B) British

C) French

13

1) **C** - The French set up trading posts to buy and ship furs.

2) **A** - The Spanish founded St. Augustine, Florida.

3) **B** - The British granted land for a prison colony in Georgia.

4) **A** - The Spanish colonies' economic focus was on ranching and mining.

5) **C** - The French built outposts on the Great Lakes and the Mississippi River.

6) **B** - The British elected assemblies and governors had weak link to European power.

1) When was slavery legal in the U.S.A.?

2) What were the rights of people held in slavery?

3) Who favored slavery?

4) The North and South had many disagreements in the early 1800s. They disagreed on tariffs, new states entering the Union, and moral issues. What war resulted from these disagreements?

1) Slavery was legal from colonial times (mid-1600s) until the Emancipation Proclamation (1863) and the end of the Civil War (1865).

2) People held in slavery did not have rights. They had to work their whole lives for owners who paid them no wages. They were not allowed to learn to read or write. Their children were often sold. Slavery was cruel and barbaric.

3) Southern slave owners who profited from the labor of slaves favored keeping slavery legal.

4) The Civil War (1861-1865)

"I want to move west, out to the Ohio country. But the _____ of 1763 makes it illegal for me to go. And this new law, _____ , makes me pay taxes on all printed papers."

— *Massachusetts farmer, 1765*

"I want to move west, out to the Ohio country. But the **Proclamation** of 1763 makes it illegal for me to go. And this new law, **the Stamp Act**, makes me pay taxes on all printed papers."

– *Massachusetts farmer, 1765*

Explain:

1) Boston Tea Party

2) The Intolerable Acts

1) Colonists disguised as Indians dumped the British East India Company's tea in Boston Harbor to protest taxes.

2) The Intolerable Acts closed the port of Boston and placed Boston under military rule.

Explain the importance of
President Andrew Jackson.

Andrew Jackson was the first president to be elected after many states allowed free white men without property to vote. Jacksonian Democracy is a term used in American politics to describe the period when the "common man" participated in the government. His presidency was known for the Indian Removal Act and the growth of democracy.

Discuss these factors that led to sectional division:

- **Compromise of 1850**
- **Fugitive Slave Act**
- **Dred Scott decision**

- **Compromise of 1850:** New Mexico, Nevada, Arizona, and Utah became organized territories without mention of slavery. Slave trade was abolished in Washington, D.C., but slavery was still permitted. California was declared a free state.

- **Fugitive Slave Act:** This act required citizens to assist in the recovery of fugitive slaves and denied a fugitive's right to a jury trial.

- **Dred Scott decision:** The Supreme Court held that a person held in slavery was property, not a citizen, and had no rights under the Constitution. The Supreme Court also ruled that the federal government did not have the power to prohibit slavery in new territories.

Each factor below caused **sectional division**. Explain each.

- **Kansas-Nebraska Act**
- **Formation of Republican Party**
- **John Brown's Raid**

- **Kansas-Nebraska Act:** This act allowed citizens in these territories to vote on the question of allowing slavery. It repealed the Missouri Compromise.

- **Formation of Republican Party:** Opponents of the Kansas-Nebraska Act organized to fight against slavery. They formed a new political party.

- **John Brown's Raid:** In 1859, abolitionist John Brown led 21 men on a raid of the federal arsenal at Harper's Ferry, Virginia, to try to get weapons to give to slaves.

Civil War

	Union	Confederacy
North or South		
President		
Key General		

Civil War

	Union	Confederacy
North or South	North	South
President	Abraham Lincoln	Jefferson Davis
Key General	Ulysses S. Grant	Robert E. Lee

1) What was Reconstruction?

2) When was Reconstruction?

3) Define carpetbaggers and scalawags.

4) What were the goals of Reconstruction?

1) Reconstruction was the period of reunion and change following the Civil War.

2) 1865-1877

3) Carpetbaggers were Northerners who settled in the South. Scalawags were Southerners in the Republican Party.

4) Reconstruction rebuilt the South's economy and changed laws to allow more rights for African-American citizens.

Explain the **Emancipation Proclamation**.

President Abraham Lincoln issued the **Emancipation Proclamation**, the document that freed all the slaves, on January 1, 1863.

What were the **Federalist Papers?**

The Federalist Papers were articles written for a New York newspaper to show support for the ratification of the Constitution. John Hamilton, James Madison, and John Jay published more than 80 essays defending the new Constitution.

1) What ideas from the Enlightenment helped form the basis of U.S. government?

2) Name and describe the three parts of the Declaration of Independence.

24

1) The idea of natural, human rights

Rebellion is justified if the ruler no longer has the consent of the people.

2) **The Preamble:** all are created equal and have the rights to life, liberty, and the pursuit of happiness

List of grievances: listed the British king's violations of the American colonists' rights

Statement of separation: the U.S. declared that it was now a free nation, no longer a British colony

For hundreds of years immigrants have been arriving in the U.S. Each group of immigrants changes the U.S. and is changed by life in the U.S.

How is each factor below affected by immigration?

1) Housing
2) Voting
3) Education
4) Language
5) Labor practices
6) Religion

1) Housing shortages may result. Large groups may be housed in crowded and unsanitary conditions. Housing styles may change as immigrants build houses that resemble those of their homeland.

2) Large ethnic groups create new voting blocs. Politicians may seek to influence these groups and change the focus of their campaigns.

3) Schools may be ill-equipped to meet the needs of new immigrants with other languages and cultures. Schools are enriched by the variety of new ideas.

4) The English language expands, as some words for foods, objects, or ideas from the immigrants' languages become a part of English.

5) New immigrants may be willing to work in jobs traditionally unattractive to long-time citizens and to work for lower wages. Highly skilled immigrants seeking opportunity bring advanced skills to the economy. Long-time citizens may resent immigrants' employment or appreciate immigrants' skills.

6) Differences in religion may cause tension with current citizens. Religious institutions change and expand to accommodate new beliefs.

What was the goal of the women's rights reform movement in the mid 1800s? Include names of prominent people who influenced this movement.

Women sought equal legal rights, including the right to own property and vote. Elizabeth Cady Stanton organized the 1848 Seneca Falls Convention, the first women's rights convention. Susan B. Anthony supported women's right to vote and the abolition of slavery. (Women received the right to vote by constitutional amendment in 1920.)

Identify each: Alexander Hamilton or James Madison?

1) Father of the Constitution

2) Wrote most of the Federalist papers

3) Founded Federalist Party; favored strong central government

4) Founded Democratic-Republican Party; favored states' rights

5) His picture is on the $10 bill; he was the first secretary of the treasury

6) He was a president of the United States

1) James Madison - Father of the Constitution

2) Alexander Hamilton - Wrote most of the Federalist papers

3) Alexander Hamilton - Founded Federalist Party; favored strong central government

4) James Madison - Founded Democratic-Republican Party; favored states rights

5) Alexander Hamilton - His picture is on the $10 bill; he was first secretary of the treasury

6) James Madison - He was a president of the United States

What was the **Underground Railroad?**

The **Underground Railroad** was a network of people who helped slaves escape. It was not an actual railroad.

1) What is the **Trail of Tears?**

2) What was the effect of the **Indian Removal Act?**

1) In the 1830s, thousands of Cherokee Indians were forced by the U.S. government to move west. About 4,000 Cherokee Indians died during this forced migration along the trail known as the **Trail of Tears**.

2) In 1830, Native Americans signed treaties with the U.S. and ceded (gave up) their land east of the Mississippi in exchange for western lands.

Matching

1) 13th Amendment

2) 14th Amendment

3) 15th Amendment

A) guaranteed black men the right to vote

B) abolished slavery

C) gave equal protection to all persons and defined citizenship

1) 13th Amendment: **B,** abolished slavery

2) 14th Amendment: **C,** gave equal protection to all persons and defined citizenship

3) 15th Amendment: **A,** guaranteed black men the right to vote

What are some of the reasons that people migrate from one region to another?

- To escape oppression/to find freedom
- To escape poverty/to find economic opportunity
- To join family or friends in a new land
- To escape wars or prejudice
- To escape flood, drought, or overcrowding

Suppose in pre-Civil War America, imported cloth was sold for $6/bolt. Then, a new tariff added $3/bolt to the price, raising it to $9/bolt. Cloth made in America sold for $7/bolt.

Would each person favor or oppose this tariff?

1) A mill owner in the North who makes cloth

2) A seamstress in the South who buys cloth to sew clothes

3) A factory worker in the North who makes cloth at work and sews her own clothes at home

1) Favor. The higher price of imported cloth will increase the mill's sales.

2) Oppose. The cloth that used to cost $6/bolt now costs $9/bolt. The only other option still costs more.

3) Probably favor. Sewing costs rise, but this worker's job is protected.

Matching:

1) Established weak national government

2) Did not give national government power to tax

3) Demonstrated a need for strong national government

4) Supreme law of the U.S.A. today

A) Articles of Confederation

B) Constitution

C) Shay's Rebellion

1) **A,** Articles of Confederation: Established weak national government

2) **A,** Articles of Confederation: Did not give national government power to tax

3) **C,** Shay's Rebellion: Demonstrated a need for strong national government

4) **B,** Constitution: Supreme law of the U.S.A. today

Shay's Rebellion and economic problems convinced Americans that a strong national government was needed. The first document that established law, The Articles of Confederation, was replaced by the Constitution.

1) What happened at the
   Battle of Gettysburg?

2) What was the importance
   of this battle?

1) The Union General George Meade defeated the Confederate General Robert E. Lee in the Battle of Gettysburg (Pennsylvania). More men, from both sides, fought and died in this battle than in any other Civil War battle.

2) This battle was the turning point in the Civil War. Confederate soldiers retreated to the South. They never attacked the North again, and they surrendered less than two years later.

Does each phrase describe
George Washington, Thomas Jefferson, or both men?

1) the commander in chief of American armies during the American Revolution

2) from Virginia; slave owner

3) founded the University of Virginia

4) the third president of the U.S.A.

5) an author of the Declaration of Independence

6) he rejected notion of becoming king of the U.S.A.; favored democracy instead

1) George Washington - the commander in chief of American armies during the American Revolution

2) both men - from Virginia; slave owner

3) Thomas Jefferson - he founded the University of Virginia

4) Thomas Jefferson - the third president of the U.S.A.

5) Thomas Jefferson - an author of the Declaration of Independence

6) George Washington - he rejected notion of becoming king of the U.S.A.; favored democracy instead

1) List the duties of each branch of government.

2) Why is power divided in the United States?

1) **Legislative Branch** - makes the laws

   Executive Branch - enforces the laws

   Judicial Branch - interprets the law and uses
   the law to decide cases

2) Power is divided to create a check and balance
   system. No one person or group has total
   control over government power.

Define Manifest Destiny.

Manifest Destiny was the belief that it was the fate of the United States to expand from the Atlantic Ocean to the Pacific Ocean. Manifest Destiny was an idea rather than a policy.

Put the following steps in order of how a bill becomes law.

1) Both House and Senate pass it.

2) House or Senate introduces it.

3) Congress may override a presidential veto.

4) Committees meet and discuss it.

5) President signs or vetoes it.

2) House or Senate introduces it.

4) Committees meet and discuss it.

1) Both House and Senate pass it.

5) President signs or vetoes it.

3) Congress may override a presidential veto.

What are some main provisions of
the Northwest Ordinance?

The Northwest Ordinance

- organized the Northwest Territory into 5 states

- allowed for public education in the territory

- prohibited slavery in the territory

- promised decent treatment for Native Americans in the territory

1) What does it mean to be an active citizen?

2) Why is it important to vote?

1) An active citizen works for the betterment of the community. He or she participates, volunteers, or works in other ways to improve life for all citizens.

2) We vote to elect representatives, to express our opinion on an issue, and to influence the direction of our community, state, or nation. Informed voters are active citizens.

1) What were the **Black Codes?**

2) What was their purpose?

1) The **Black Codes** were laws passed by many Southern legislatures after the Civil War ended.

2) The purpose of the Black Codes was to keep black citizens in a state similar to slavery. African Americans were forced to agree to manual labor contracts and set work hours. Sometimes they needed licenses to work non-farming jobs.

1) What is a **primary source?**

2) What is a **secondary source?**

1) **Primary source** - a document, record, or written account created by a person who took part in or witnessed an event; for example, George Washington's diary is a primary source for the American Revolution.

2) **Secondary source** - a written account created by a person who was not a participant or eyewitness at an event; it is written some time after the event has occurred. For example, a history textbook is a secondary source for the American Revolution.

1) What is the name of any change or addition to the Constitution of the United States?

2) Some states would not ratify the Constitution until it was amended to include citizens' rights. What is the name of these first 10 amendments that list the basic rights of American citizens?

1) amendment

2) Bill of Rights

1) What are the five rights guaranteed by the First Amendment?

2) List some constitutional rights of people accused of a crime in the U.S.A.

1) freedom of religion, freedom of speech, freedom of press, freedom of assembly, freedom of petition

2) • The right to counsel (an attorney)
   • The right to a speedy and public trial
   • The right to know the charges (the accusations)
   • The right to a trial by jury
   • The right to refuse to be a witness against oneself

Explain the lasting effects of each of the following military conquests during the Middle Ages.

1) Mongol invasions

2) Muslim conquests

1) The Mongols conquered most of Asia under Genghis and Kublai Khan. The Mongols destroyed cities they conquered and, in some cases, tried to stamp out Islam.

2) The Muslim conquests allowed Islam to spread into Africa and parts of Spain.

What was the **abolition movement?**

Who were some prominent people involved in this movement?

The abolition movement sought an end to slavery.

- Frederick Douglass escaped slavery and was an abolitionist leader.

- Harriet Tubman led slaves to freedom along the Underground Railroad.

- William Lloyd Garrison was a writer who called for slavery's end.

- Harriet Beecher Stowe authored *Uncle Tom's Cabin*, an anti-slavery novel.

Match the civilization with its description.
Maya   or   Mississippian

1) Which group played a fierce ball game similar to soccer?

2) Which culture was known for building earth mounds as tombs or for ceremonies?

3) Which culture was located in the area of the modern day United States?

4) Which civilization was located throughout northern Central America and some parts of southern Mexico?

1) Maya

2) Mississippian

3) Mississippian

4) Maya

Define

1) Monarchy

2) Constitutional monarchy

3) Absolute monarchy

1) **Monarchy** is a system of government in which **the ruler is determined by birth**; the ruler remains in office for life.

2) **Constitutional monarchy** is a system of government in which **powers of the monarch are limited** to those permitted under the laws of the nation.

3) **Absolute monarchy** is a system of government in which **a hereditary ruler controls all governmental powers**.

1) What is a compromise?

2) Match:

A) The Three-Fifths
   Compromise

B) The compromise over
   the slave trade

C) The Great Compromise

I) Congress would have two
    separate houses.

II) The method used to count
     slaves in a census for a
     state's representation in
     Congress and for taxes.

III) This would be permitted
      until 1808, then Congress
      could end it.

1) A **compromise** is an agreement. Each side makes concessions (gives up on some demands) to reach the agreement.

2) **A)** The Three-Fifths Compromise: II, The method used to count slaves in a census for a state's representation in Congress and for taxes.

   B) The compromise over the slave trade: III, This would be permitted until 1808, then Congress could end it.

   C) The Great Compromise: I, Congress would have two separate houses.

1) Jonah could work part time and make $500 this summer, or he could go to summer school. What is the opportunity cost of working part time?

2) He could work for the library or a fast food restaurant. Which job is a private sector job? What sector does the other job belong to?

1) The opportunity cost of working part time is summer school credit that he will not receive. Opportunity cost is the value that is given up when a choice is made.

2) The job at the restaurant is a private sector job. Jonah would be an employee of people who own their own business. The job at the library is a public sector job. Jonah would be a government employee.

HOLLANDAYS
Publishing Corporation

OAT

QUESTION OF THE DAY

Start each class with a question that matches the **Ohio Achievement Test Standards:**

- Generates discussion of key concepts with targeted and in-depth questions

- Written by experienced teachers

- Labeled according to the standard being addressed

- Saves time, improves classroom management, and keeps instruction and review flowing

- On transparencies in a 3-ring binder or on CD-ROM

OHIO ORDER FORM

OAT Question of the Day Transparencies

☐ Grade 7 Mathematics................ $89
☐ Grade 8 Mathematics................ $89
☐ Grade 9 Mathematics................ $89
☐ Grade 7 Language Arts............. $89
☐ Grade 8 Language Arts............. $89
☐ Grade 8 Science........................ $89
☐ Grade 7 Social Studies............. $89
☐ Grade 8 Social Studies............. $89
☐ Site License on CD-ROM (per title)..... $295
The site license includes rights to copy the CD-ROM and project/ print from the CD-ROM.

OAT Flashcards

☐ Grade 8 Social Studies.............. $8.95
☐ Grade 8 Science........................ $8.95
☐ 25 or More Sets, Each.............. $6.00

Please add 8% for shipping and handling. Minimum $8.

Phone: 800-792-3537   Fax: 937-222-2665
Order on the web @ www.hollandays.net

Dear Parents,

Here's how to use these flashcards to help your child prepare for **Ohio 8th Grade Social Studies:**

- Use the flashcards regularly. Practice 15-30 minutes each night.

- Make a checkmark on a flashcard each time your child answers that card correctly. After several sessions look for flashcards with no (or few) checkmarks. Discuss these with your child and seek help from the teacher for these skills.

- Review your child's social studies class assignments. Discuss repeated errors and focus on improving those skills.

- Read the advice to students on the reverse side of this card and urge your child to follow it.

US $8.95

ISBN 0-9769459-6-7

50895

9 780976 945963

Dear Student,
Here are some ideas to help you as you prepare for **Ohio 8th Grade Social Studies:**

- **Read the test carefully.** Don't just skim. Read the question and all responses before you answer.

- Study **maps, charts, and graphs** in your textbooks. Make sure you understand how to read each one.

- Make sure you understand how to read **timelines.**

- Seek help from a teacher or parent if you need help with any of the terms or ideas on your flashcards.

- **Use your best handwriting** on short answer and extended response questions.

- **Write thorough answers for full credit.** Short answer questions are worth two points and extended response questions are worth four points.

- **Come to the test rested and prepared.**

©2008
Hollandays
Publishing
Corporation